Contents

The Oxford Centre for Staff Development

5

riting

says

pping Writing

tute

ology

hnology

Kate Williams

Published by

THE OXFORD CENTRE FOR STAFF DEVELOPMENT

Oxford Brookes University

Gipsy Lane

Headington

Oxford

OX3 0BP

Developing Writing – Writing Essays ISBN 1 873576 40 4

British Library Cataloguing-in-Publication Data. A catalogue record for this book is available from the British Library.

Designed and Typeset in 10 on 12.5 pt Palatino and Helvetica by Lisa Hill and Thomas Nicolaou

Printed in Great Britain by

Oxonian Rewley Press Ltd

Oxford

Printed on paper produced from sustainable forests.

1   Essay writing in focus

How do I write a good essay? That's the billion dollar question to which you want an answer – which is why you're thumbing through this guide. Here goes.

To write a good essay, you need to focus

- outwards – on what the task is, and the guidance you have been given or can find as to what is expected of you

- inwards – on how you are going to set about meeting those requirements.

Before you start working, you need to be absolutely clear about your answers to these questions:

What exactly do you have to produce? What content? What form?

Why are you writing this essay? What do you want out of it?

Who is it for? What does your reader want to see in it?

The second set of questions are key to your success in organizing yourself to carry out a sensible programme of work within the constraint of time.

How do you set about it? How do you structure the essay?

Where do you work at each stage?

When do you do each stage? When are the deadlines?

This booklet is structured around a search for answers to these questions. The plan below shows how this is organized.

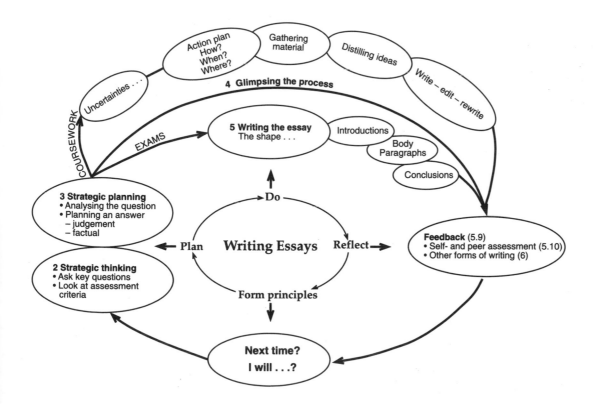

1.1 How to use this guide

Study the plan of the guide, starting with **Strategic thinking** (Chapter 2). This chapter takes a close look at the assessment criteria that will apply to your finished product.

Which chapter you go on to next depends on

- your personal approach to essay writing

- the point you are at in the essay writing cycle.

Strategic planning (Chapter 3) suggests a systematic approach to analysing the question and planning an outline answer.

Glimpsing the process (Chapter 4) takes an overview of the entire process of writing, and **Writing the essay** (Chapter 5) deals with the nitty gritty of putting an essay together – writing paragraphs, introductions and conclusions, and making sure the whole thing works to build your case and record your researches in a systematic and convincing way. You can turn to particular sections of this whenever you need to.

Chapter 6, **Essays are not the only way . . .**, looks at how to apply the principles of essay writing to other writing tasks you might be set.

2 Strategic thinking

2.1 Ask key questions

What exactly do you have to produce?

Why are you writing this essay? What is it designed to achieve?

Who is it for?

These key questions prompt you to look outwards, to the context in which you are writing the essay.

What exactly do you have to produce?

'Write an essay' is a shorthand that makes certain assumptions: that the piece of writing will

- be of a certain length

- have a particular structure and layout

- address a specific question or aspect of a topic

- be written in a formal academic style.

Fortunately, most tutors agree on the general qualities of a good essay – 'well structured', 'answers the question'. Unfortunately, they differ from one discipline to another and from one tutor to another about what a well structured answer is, and the style in which it should be written. Often you only find this out when you get your essay back – marked and assessed. If only you had known before what you know now . . .

Why are you writing this essay?

There will always be

- external reasons: course requirements, an assessment schedule, a notion on the tutor's part of the academic and critical skills you should be developing

- a private purpose: a means by which you make sense of what you have learnt, and develop the skills to write about it.

This dual – or conflicting – purpose is probably what makes essay writing so daunting: exhilarating and exciting when it goes well, depressing and miserable when it does not.

Who is your essay for?

Yourself? Your tutor? Fellow students? Posterity? It helps if you can define your audience. Some tasks build in an audience – you have to share a piece of work with a group, or write it as if for publication in a particular periodical, or whatever. All this makes it easier to know what tone to adopt, the level to pitch it at, and so on. Most essay writing tasks, however, do not specify an audience and so a rule of thumb can be helpful.

A rule of thumb on audience

If you have not been given any specific guidance about your audience, write as if you are addressing someone with the same experience and knowledge of the general subject area as yourself, but who has not yet covered this topic/module/course. In this way you will not be tempted to

- talk up, using fancy language designed to impress

- talk down, with an inappropriately informal or chatty style.

Talk on the level, using clear, simple language, and draw on the specialist jargon and conventions of your subject when you need to.

Some of the conventions of academic essay writing make more sense seen in this light too: your reader will want to see the evidence for the points you make, and will appreciate the references that will enable them to go and check it out for themselves. There's more on this in Chapter 5.

To make sure you are on track when you set out to write an essay for your tutor in your subject, look ahead to the end of the assessment process before you start on your essay. Find out how your essay will be assessed. What exactly is your tutor looking for?

2.2   Looking at assessment criteria: the tutor's perspective

What guidance do you have as to what is expected of you? Have you been given

- printed sheets with explicit assessment criteria?

- a chat from the tutor, formal or informal?

- written advice in a course handbook?

- no guidance at all?

The extracts below give a taste of what different tutors look for in their students' essays.

Activity

1   Look closely at the three extracts below, and draw up a list of criteria for essay writing on which you think these tutors from different disciplines would agree.

2   Draw up a list of criteria you think will apply to the next essay you write. Decide on the degree of detail you will find helpful.

If you can, work with someone else on this activity. Two heads are better than one.

Extract 1

This tutor is very clear about what he expects – and does not expect – to find in a good essay in his subject (geology).

What makes a good essay?

What should the essay contain

1 legible handwriting or typed/word processed text
2 *all* the relevant information to *answer* the question
3 a clear structure with introduction, description, summary
4 clear, concise grammar
5 illustrations (with derivation)
6 list of properly quoted references
7 examples from the trip, clearly explained!

What shouldn't be present!

A waffle, repetition and poor grammar
B *unreferenced* information, eg from books
C meaningless diagrams
D poor organization
E irrelevant information

He uses the same headings in his rating system when he marks the essay.

*=v.good   ✔=good   ?=ok(fair)   x=poor   — =nothing

1	2	3	4	5	6	7	A	B	C	D	E	Mark/Grade
✔	*	✔	✔	?	—	x?	*	—	x	✔	✔	low B+

HR   ANSWERS QUESTION QUITE WELL!

       well written, makes good sense, well organized
Needs headings?   Seriously lacks:-
        illustration of forms of mineralizations
        maps
        reference to information sources
        details of minerals
        why not economic now?
        discussion
    Good points –statistics on output etc.

He prefers to keep his criteria and marking in an informal, handwritten style. The application is nonetheless rigorous.

Extract 2

This marking sheet for an essay in town planning shows the qualities the marker will be looking for, the rating scale and the comments together on a standard sheet. The comments show how the tutor applies the criteria to a particular piece of work.

ASSIGNMENT 2: ESSAY

This report has been assessed on the following criteria (see pp.45–6 of the handbook):

	Very Good	Good	Average	Poor	Very Poor
1. ESSAY STRUCTURE *It had a structure, true, not entirely appropriate to question!*		✓			
2. DEVELOPMENT OF ARGUMENT *I found it somewhat confused at times. A lot of key points not here.*			✓		
3. QUANTITY/QUALITY OF READING *You made use of 2 – but could have usefully looked at others*			✓		
4. BIBLIOGRAPHY/SOURCES *Not very well cited – errors and incomplete refs.*				✓	
5. QUALITY OF WRITTEN ENGLISH *I think you ought to try to write shorter sentences – sometimes a little laboured – clumsy.*				✓	
6. PRESENTATIONS/ILLUSTRATIONS *Nicely word processed.*	✓				
7. SIGNS OF ORIGINALITY *Average.*					

8. GENERAL COMMENTS
I didn't feel you really got to grips with this – too long a preamble – (not necessary) and you said little about the specific impact of planning devices like CDAs, partnership deals or indirect effects of wider policies.

ASSESSED MARK 58
- deduction for:
SEMINAR _____
LATENESS _____

STUDENT: _____
ASSESSOR: *LH* _____
FINAL MARK 58%

Extract 3

In this extract from an essay assessment sheet for psychology, the marker makes written comments only on points that are individual to the particular student. This department has taken the view that since most lecturers' comments fall into clearly defined categories, it is more effective to have a detailed breakdown of what each of the headings means, and to tick the student's performance under each criterion.

Essay Assessment Sheet

		Marker		
Name			Mark	
Date in	Date back			
Writer's Specific Requests For Feedback				
Marker's General View Of The Work				

Rating Scale	Excellent	Very good	Satisfactory	Needs some more work	Needs much more work
INTRODUCTION TO THE ESSAY					
Interpretation of title and introduction	....	....	....	....	....
DEVELOPMENT OF THE ESSAY					
Logical development	....	....	....	....	....
Insight and originality	....	....	....	....	....
Subject relevance	....	....	....	....	....
Use of sources	....	....	....	....	....
Use of evidence	....	....	....	....	....
Understanding of topic	....	....	....	....	....
Constructive critical analysis	....	....	....	....	....
CONCLUSION TO THE ESSAY	....	....	....	....	....
OTHER FEATURES					
Presentation of references	....	....	....	....	....
Legibility	....	....	....	....	....
Spelling	....	....	....	....	....
Grammar & Syntax	....	....	....	....	....
Style	....	....	....	....	....
Length	....	....	....	....	....
Overall presentation	....	....	....	....	....

SPECIFIC ASPECTS OF YOUR ESSAY ....that the marker likes	SPECIFIC ASPECTS OF YOUR ESSAY ...... that need more work

---

INTRODUCTION TO THE ESSAY
'Interpretation of title and introduction'

Excellent/Very good — Introduction shows a sound grasp of the question and provides a clear outline of the scope of the essay

Satisfactory — Introduction rambles and scope of essay not defined.

Needs more/much more work — Launches straight in with no attempt to introduce and define the topic Questions may have been misunderstood.

DEVELOPMENT OF THE ESSAY
'Logical development'

Excellent/Very good — Develops a logical argument and ideas clearly.

Satisfactory — Could be better organised by sequencing some of the material more appropriately.

Needs more/much more work — Fails to develop a clear theme or line of argument.

'Use of sources'

Excellent/Very good — Critical and wide-range use of relevant literature

Satisfactory — Likely sources and material covered.

Needs more/much more work — Little evidence of supportive reading. Inadequate preparation.

'Understanding of topic'

Excellent/Very good — Well argued. All main issues explored and evaluated and conclusion justified.

Satisfactory — Most main issues explored. Some analysis and critical evaluation.

Needs more/much more work — Work is descriptive, accepting and/or one-sided with little analysis or criticism.

CONCLUSION TO THE ESSAY

Excellent/Very good — Good concluding section which draws together the various important points made.

Satisfactory — Rather brief and formalised conclusion

Need more/much more work — The essay abruptly and/or simply rephrases the introduction.

Explicit criteria like these help you to see what your tutor wants in your essay. If you have been given assessment criteria, use them to help you plan and write your essay. If you have not, use the list you drew up in the activity on p. 8 to help you.

2.3   The learning cycle: the student's perspective

What do you want from your essay?

A good mark, of course, and . . . personal satisfaction? It's a good feeling when you find you've gained

- some knowledge of your subject

- understanding of the implications or uses of this knowledge

- the ability to move around other people's ideas, to question, weigh one against another, examine the evidence, investigate your own attitudes, and find you have a view . . .

- some skill in essay writing.

In short, when you've put that amount of effort into an essay, you want to feel you've moved on in some way, and that you can use each essay to further your learning process, ready for next time. This, of course, is what your tutor is looking for too. Your purpose in writing the essay and your tutor's purpose in assessing it may be closer than you thought. It all depends on agreeing on the rules of the game, the first and last of which are to

answer the question set.

3 Strategic planning

3.1 What is the question asking?

Imagine for a moment that you are the tutor or examiner who, every year, has to set a question on the same topic for the same course.

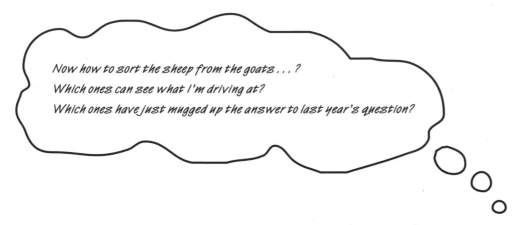

Now how to sort the sheep from the goats . . . ?

Which ones can see what I'm driving at?

Which ones have just mugged up the answer to last year's question?

You do it by setting questions on different *aspects* of the same topic. This will quickly show you which students have an understanding of the subject. They will

* write in depth on a particular aspect

* think flexibly about the subject by looking at it from a new angle

* include only material relevant to the question you have set.

The answers from students who have a shaky grasp of the topic will

* be general 'all I know about . . .' answers

* show no new thinking

* contain irrelevant material

and there will always be a few who write last year's answer to this year's question.

Activity

Below are two questions from a public policy exam paper. What are they about?

ESSAY 1

Account for the emergence of the policy of privatization developed by successive Conservative governments during the 1980s.

ESSAY 2

Critically discuss the view that the policy on privatization promoted by successive Conservative governments since 1979 has been a success.

The questions are both, of course, *about* the privatization policies of various Conservative governments – but there the similarities end. The questions contain all the clues you need to write well planned, well structured, relevant answers. All you need to do is to unpack each question systematically to see exactly what it is asking – and then answer it!

3.2 How to analyse the question: a five-step plan

Here is a systematic way of unpacking or analysing an essay question. Try it on these essay titles.

ESSAY 1

Account for the emergence of the policy of privatization developed by successive Conservative governments during the 1980s.

Step 1

Identify the subject

This is the topic on the syllabus or course outline – the knowledge base. If the subject is hard to identify, try this:

- Read the question, look up and ask yourself, 'What, in a nutshell, is this question *about?*'

- If the question was on an exam paper and someone asked you which questions you'd done, you'd say, 'I did the one on . . .'

Usually, it's not a problem.

Here it is the *policy of privatization.*

Step 2

Identify the instruction

This is the word that tells you **how** you are expected to write. Are you asked to explain? Compare and contrast? Account for? Evaluate? Discuss? Each of these will require a different style of essay.

The instruction here is to *account for.*

Step 3

Identify the key aspect(s) this particular essay is asking for. These are the key words of the question, the ones you plan your answer around, and stick to from the first paragraph to the last.

The key aspect here is the *emergence* of the policy of privatization.

Step 4

Are there other **significant words** to take into account to help you define the scope of your answer?

The significant words here are *successive Conservative governments* and *during the 1980s.* There are two points here: the different administrations (how did they differ?), and the time span – the 1980s only.

Step 5

Ask questions about the question. The essay is about *the policy of privatization.* What was this? What was its scope? A definition is needed here. *Emergence* is an interesting word – suggesting a process rather than an event. How did these policies emerge – as a whole, or piecemeal? What pressures were at work? *Successive* is also worth pausing over: which administrations were these? How did they differ – in political make-up, outlook, emphasis, etc.

How to analyse the question

1 Identify the subject.   Box it.

2 Identify the instruction.   Underline it.

3 Identify the key aspect(s).   Double underline.

4 Look for other significant words that help to
  pinpoint the scope of your answer.   Use a wiggly line.

5 Ask questions about words and phrases in the question.
  What does this word mean? What does this imply?   Scribble, annotate.

Activity

Copy out the question in Essay 1 and follow the five steps to analyse it, using the annotations in the box. Have a go before you look at the version below.

The question in Essay 1 now looks like this:

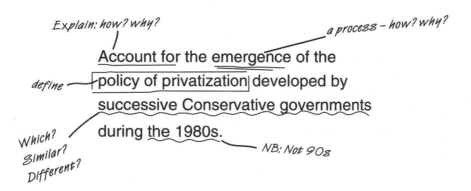

Explain: how? why?

a process – how? why?

Account for the emergence of the

define —— policy of privatization developed by

successive Conservative governments

Which?
Similar?
Different?   during the 1980s.

NB: Not 90s

Activity

Analyse the title of Essay 2, below, in the same way, following steps 1 to 5. Then check your analysis with the one at the end of the chapter.

ESSAY 2

Critically discuss the view that the policy on privatization promoted by successive Conservative governments since 1979 has been a success.

A close analysis of the question helps you to pinpoint what *this* question is asking. You will have to draw on the same core of knowledge to answer questions on the same topic – but you will have to show this knowledge in very different ways.

Essay 1 is asking you to explain a complex process.

Essay 2 is asking you to question the evidence for a view, and, in your conclusion, to give your own view.

3.3 How to plan an outline answer

Use this visual analysis of the question as a basis for an instant outline answer. You can change it later, but draw it now when the bits of the title are fresh in your mind.

Essay 1 shapes up like this.

Account for the emergence of the policy of privatization developed by successive Conservative governments during the 1980s

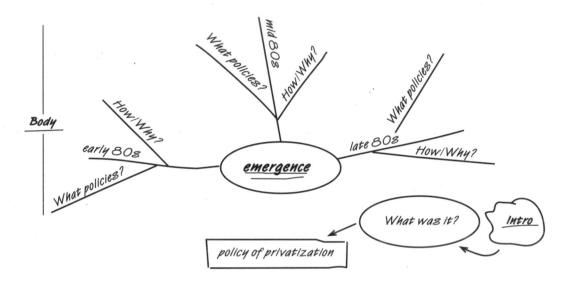

Conclusion: *Common thread/most powerful factor + look ahead?*

How to draw an instant plan

1   Take a whole side of A4.

2   Give yourself two minutes.

3   Do several quick sketches.

4   Use only the words and phrases in the question.

5   Show links.

6   Look for a pattern or structure.

This will give you

• a focus for your researches

• an overall structure for your essay, plus ideas for the introduction and conclusion

• possible clusters of paragraphs.

As you get going on the work for your essay, all this might change, but it is much better to start with something than with nothing.

An instant plan will go a long way towards ensuring that your answer will have the two key qualities on which tutors agree. Your essay will

- **'answer the question'.** By using the words and phrases from the title as a basis for your instant plan, you will have to focus on **what** to address – the key points in this particular essay

- be **'well structured'.** An instant plan starts you thinking about **how** to organize your material.

Activity

Draw an instant plan for an answer to Essay 2. Be disciplined about not looking at the version below until you have had a go.

This essay plan is much easier to draw than that for Essay 1. You work back from the conclusion: was the policy a success or not? Or rather, to what extent was it successful or not?

<u>Critically discuss</u> the <u>view</u> that the [policy on privatization] promoted by successive Conservative governments since 1979 has been a <u>success</u>.

Introduction:

Critically discuss
Needs a judgement

Argument and evidence

Argument and evidence

policy on privatization

Yes

success?

No

Argument and evidence (i)

Argument and evidence (ii)

Conclusion:

Yes, 100%
brilliant

Very successful,
minor hitches

Neither good
nor bad

Overall unsuccessful.
Some good features

No, total
disaster, 0%

X   X   X

Watch out if you find yourself assuming one of the positions marked with a large X. You need to be very sure of your ground to take either of the extremes.

- Avoid the extremes. The issue is complex. Can your answer really be that simple?

- Avoid the middle – sitting on the fence. Do you really have no view at all after studying the subject?

You can use this outline as a model for any essay where you have to make a judgement.

3.4   Types of question and styles of answer

Below is a review of the two essay titles you analysed above. Take a good look at the different writing tasks implied by each.

What do I have to do?

ANALYSIS	Essay 1		Essay 2
1 Subject	policy of privatization	← *same* →	policy of privatization
2 Instruction	'Account for' Explain how and why? Point and illustration ⟶ a factual essay	← *different* →	'Critically discuss' Scrutinize assertion Use argument and evidence ⟶ a judgement essay
3 Key aspects	'emergence' of policy – how? why?	← *different* →	'success' of policy – to what extent was it? or not?
4 Significant words	'successive Conservative governments' 1980s	← *same* → ← *different* →	'successive Conservative governments' since 1979
5 Question . . .	define . . . ponder . . .		pinpoint . . .

The message (again): these titles are asking for **completely different essays.** You may even be beginning to sympathize with the tutor/examiner who gets the same 'all I know about . . .' answer for each. The difference in content, as we have seen, stems from the key aspect. The difference in writing style stems from the **instruction**: 'account for' and 'critically discuss'.

Some instructions ask you to make a **judgement** of some sort: *How far? To what extent? Should . . . ? Discuss the view.*

Others are asking for a more **factual** treatment: *Outline, Account for, Explain.*

This is, of course, an oversimplification – but a useful one, because instructions are the words that

- tell you how to write; the style of the essay

- suggest what you write; an outline structure for your essay.

> ### Activity
> Read the essay titles below. Divide the titles into two groups:
> 1 titles in which you need to make a judgement of some sort
> 2 titles which ask for a factual account.

1   Was Malthus right on population?

2   Outline the possible approaches to identifying travel needs in rural areas. What do you consider to be their relative merits?

3   It is a commonplace observation that workers dislike and resist change in the workplace. How far do you think this is a rational response to their economic position and how far simply a result of the mismanagement of change?

4   Examine the roots of the debt problem in the developing countries and the possible solutions to the problem.

5   Discuss the factors which a manager would need to consider when designing either a pay/salary structure or a payment/reward system for a hospitality organization.

6   To what extent has technological change contributed to the changing industrial structure of the UK in the twentieth century?

7   What are the reasons for staffing problems within the hotel and catering industry? Suggest ways in which these might be overcome.

8   Compare and contrast the formal garden design of seventeenth-century France and the English Landscape movement of the eighteenth century, indicating what relevance, if any, these might have for modern urban design.

9   To what extent has the Conservative government's programme of trade union reform since 1979 been a success?

10 'A full understanding of a country's political system is impossible without the use of comparison.' Discuss.

11 Outline the main dimensions of change experienced in the UK conurbations in the last 40 years and discuss the extent to which these changes have come about as a result of public planning policies.

12 How significant are political parties in American politics?

13 Why do some firms take over others?

Do you agree with this division?

1   Answers will be structured around a **judgement** in essays 1, 3, 6, 9, 10 and 12. Instructions that point to judgement essays include: How far. . . ? To what extent. . . ? Do you consider. . . ?, and How . . . ?, as in How significant. . . ? How successful. . . ? Many judgement essay titles simply pose a direct question: Is there such a thing as trade union freedom? Was Malthus right about population?

2   Answers with less scope for argument and interpretation – **factual** – are 2, 4, 5, 7, 8, 11 and 13. Instructions that point to factual essays include: Outline, Compare and contrast, Examine. Again, some direct questions require factual treatment: How. . . ?, What are. . . ?, Why. . . ?

Which were the tricky ones?

- Discuss: this can point to a judgement essay, as in (10) above, or it can be asking for a factual presentation, as in (5). Here the scope for your views is very limited.

- Two-part questions: these usually have a factual first part (outline, define, explain), with an evaluation or judgement to be made in the second part.

3.5   A closer look at judgement essays

Activity: Defining

Look back to the instructions to the judgement essays you identified in the activity on pp. 18-19.

- List them.

- Try to define briefly what each means.

- Think about what this implies for the structure and style of the essay.

Activity: Making judgements

Make a snap judgement in answer to each of the following questions on the sliding scale below. It makes it more interesting if you can compare your position with other people's.

Yes, totally, 100%.		No, not at all, 0%.

To what extent/how far do you agree that

1   students should pay for the cost of their higher education?

2   the private lives of public figures should remain private?

3   your parents had more opportunities than you do?

4   the policy of privatization promoted by successive Conservative governments has been a success?

5   Malthus was right about population?

You will probably have started out confidently on these questions, been hesitant about no. 4 and been stumped by the last. 'But I don't know anything about this!' you say. Quite right – this is where you need some knowledge. Personal experience is enough to support your own opinion in the first three questions, but in the last two you do not know enough about the subject to express a view in which you can have confidence. You need to go off and come back with some knowledge to draw on as evidence for your views. You will then have an *informed* view, which you can develop through the *argument* of your essay. Chapter 5 considers the practicalities of this.

When you've done the work and are ready to write your essay, you will come back to your early thoughts and outline plan with a different eye. You will now have an informed view, and need to organize your material to structure this. You will need to work on your plan.

How to work on your plan

1 **Jot down points**, thoughts, examples, studies, ideas as you come across them. Ideally, attach them to the right bits of the instant plan, but if you've left lots of space you can move them around later.

And then
　　one day
　　　　as the deadline approaches
　　　　　　　and you've read all the books
　　　　　　　　　　and you've thought all the thoughts
　　　　　　　and you can't put it off any more . . .
(There's more about this in Chapter 4.)

2 **Decide on your conclusion.** You can always change your mind, but start out with an end in mind. Mark your position on a sliding scale

Yes,		No,
100%	Don't know	not at all

and avoid the extremes and the mid-point.

3 **Outline the body** of the essay. Work out the **major sections:** points for and against, key arguments and evidence.

It's fine to have

- more points on one side than the other

- points that can be argued both ways

- strong views – as long as you show what they are based on and consider the counter-arguments.

4 **Decide on your introduction.** This may now be easier than you thought. Is there

- a term to define?

- a theory to explain?

- a limit to set on the scope of your essay?

5 **Go back to the body: work out the paragraphs.** There should be

- one point per paragraph

- evidence and illustration to support it.

How to work on your plan

1 Jot down points.

2 Decide on your conclusion.

3 Outline the body: major sections.

4 Decide on your introduction.

5 Go back to the body: work out the paragraphs.

Building a judgement essay

Look back at the last two questions in the **Making Judgements** activity above. The first you analysed in Section 3.2. In full these questions are:

Critically discuss the view that the policy on privatization promoted by successive Conservative governments since 1979 has been a success.

and

Was Malthus right about population?

You have got your conclusion marked on the sliding scale. What do you do in the rest of the essay?

In a judgement essay,

you have to show that you	you do this
• know what the subject under discussion is:	in the **introduction** by • defining and explaining key terms

: what Malthus' theory about population was
: what these privatization policies were

| • know and understand the main opposing views and interpretations | in the **body** by
• presenting the arguments and evidence to support both sides |

: main theories/theorists who think Malthus was/was not right
: main interpretations of these policies and reactions to them

| • can make a judgement about the validity of the different interpretations. | in the **conclusion** by
• showing where you stand in the debate: which arguments you find most persuasive and best grounded in evidence. |

:how persuasive you find the different views on whether or not Malthus was/these policies were right.

A judgement essay is one on issues about which people can and do hold different views. For you as a writer, all judgement essays ask you to do much the same thing: to scrutinize and weigh the evidence for – or for and against – a view or argument, and to conclude by showing where you stand in the debate and why. You should be able to mark your position on a sliding scale, somewhere between the two extremes:

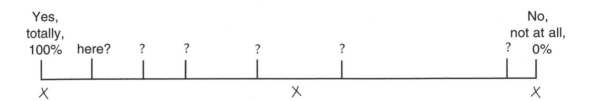

Remember the no-go areas, marked X:

Developing Writing-Writing Essays

1 Beware of sitting on the fence! Do you really have no views at all? Or haven't you understood the debate? If the issue really is finely balanced, say so explicitly. You will still probably come down more on one side than the other.

2 Avoid the extremes, unless you are very sure of your ground. No side or factor has a monopoly of right – even if you can't see how anyone could possibly have different views to your own.

The fact that the question is asked at all means that it is debatable. So debate it.

3.6　How to plan a judgement essay: Blueprint 1

Below is a summary of the approach to planning judgement essays outlined in this chapter.

1　Analyse the question

How to analyse the question

1 Identify the subject.	Box it.
2 Identify the instruction.	Underline it.
3 Identify the key aspect(s).	Double underline.
4 Look for other significant words that help to pinpoint the scope of your answer.	Use a wiggly line.
5 Ask questions about words and phrases in the question What does this word mean? What does this imply?	Scribble, annotate.

Was Malthus right on population?
— What were his theories?
Yes/No: judgement
Main interpretations? evidence?

2   Plan an outline answer

How to draw an instant plan

1 Take a whole side of A4.

2 Give yourself two minutes.

3 Do several quick sketches.

4 Use only the words and phrases in the question.

5 Show links.

6 Look for a pattern or structure.

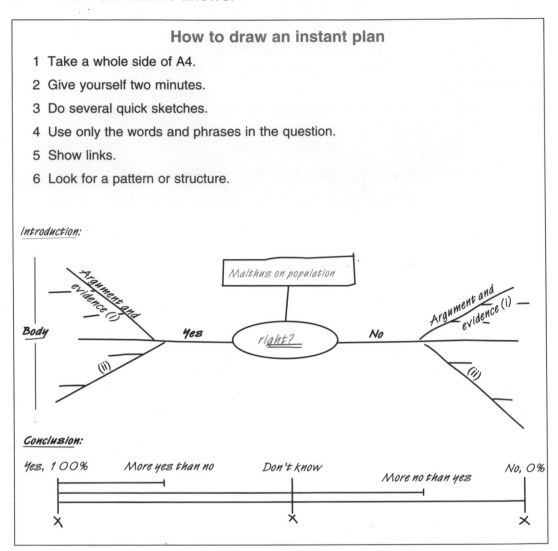

3   Work on your plan

How to work on your plan

1 Jot down points.

2 Decide on your conclusion.

3 Outline the body: major sections.

4 Decide on your introduction.

5 Go back to the body: work out the paragraphs.

Now you're ready to roll. A plan should help you write, not be another burden.

> **Activity**
>
> Try this approach to planning another judgement essay, taking a title from the list of titles on p. 19.
>
> Have a go at adding some content. It doesn't matter if you don't know anything about the subject – make it up, to get some points in the body.

3.7   A closer look at factual essays

The temptation to write 'all I know about' answers is often even stronger in factual essays than in judgement ones. People frequently respond as if they thought: 'They want the facts? They can have them.'

But they don't, and you will be penalized for writing general all-I-know-about answers. So what are you supposed to do with a factual question?

> **Activity: Defining**
>
> Look back at the instructions (e.g., outline, compare and contrast) to the essays you identified as asking for a 'factual' style in the activity on p. 19.
>
> • List them.
>
> • Try to define briefly what each means.
>
> • Think about what this implies for how you write – the structure and style of the essay. What do you have to show you can do in a 'factual' essay?

Following instructions

It is crucial to follow the instruction in factual essays because

- the range of instructions is much greater – for example, *outline, explain, evaluate, compare and contrast* – and each requires quite a different outcome in the essay

- the range in the amount of structuring you are given in the question is much greater.

As a result, 'factual' essays are often harder to plan and write.

The question may be **direct and open.**

A1 **Why do some firms take over others?**

A2 **Discuss the factors which a manager would need to consider when designing either a pay/salary structure or a payment/reward system for a hospitality organization**.

Or it may be **highly structured and focused.**

B1 **Compare and contrast the formal garden design of seventeenth-century France and the English Landscape movement of the eighteenth century, indicating what relevance, if any, these might have for modern urban design**.

B2 **Compare and contrast shade plants and CAM plants, with particular reference to their water regimes**.

Or it may be in **two parts – part factual, part judgement.**

C1 **Outline possible approaches to identifying travel needs in rural areas. What do you consider to be their relative merits?**

C2 **Outline the main dimensions of change experienced in the UK conurbations in the last 40 years and discuss the extent to which these changes have come about as a result of public planning policies.**

> ### Activity: Following instructions
>
> 1 The first essay question in each pair above gets the treatment below. Look at each one carefully, and, where you can, add some content to the skeleton.
>
> 2 Do the same thing yourself for the second question in each pair (A2, B2, C2).

As with judgement essays, once you have an outline plan, you then need to research and work on the material for your essay before you come back to your outline to develop it into a detailed plan.

A1: Why do some firms take over others?

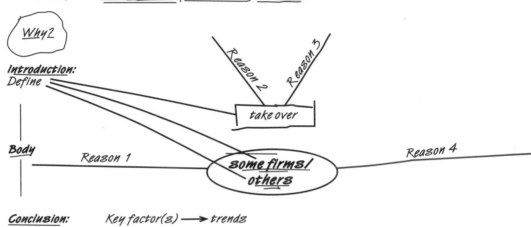

B1: Compare and contrast the formal garden design of seventeenth-century France and the English landscape movement of the eighteenth century, indicating what relevance, if any, these might have for modern urban design.

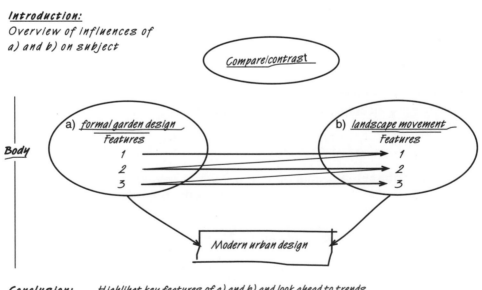

C1: <u>Outline</u> possible approaches to <u>identifying travel needs</u> in <u>rural areas</u>.
What do you consider to be their <u>relative merits</u>?

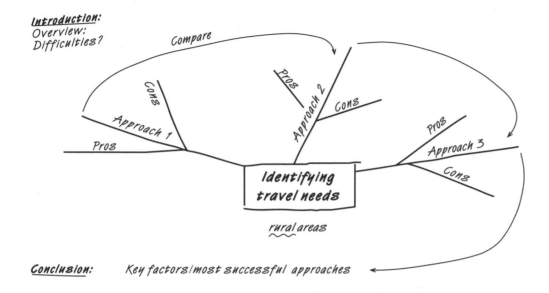

Introduction:
Overview:
Difficulties?

Compare

Cons

Approach 1

Pros

Pros

Approach 2

Cons

Pros

Approach 3

Cons

**Identifying
travel needs**

rural areas

Conclusion: Key factors/most successful approaches

How to work on your plan

The stages are the same for any essay, but you may find it better to try a different order in factual essays – because you have to look harder for your conclusion. Try the following order.

1 **Jot down points,** thoughts, examples, studies, ideas.

2 **Outline the body: major sections**

Use the words and phrases in the question for your main headings. In some essays you will have a lot to go on (as in B and C above), sometimes very little, as in A).

3 **Work on the body: plan the structure**

Think about how you will

- link points

- develop points: explain the consequences, effects or implications of the points you have made. Use illustrations to support each one.

- order your points. These will become your paragraphs. There is more about this in Chapter 5: Writing the essay.

4 **Decide on your introduction**

This is often quite straightforward. You may need to

- explain what words and phrases in the question mean, or how you will be using them

- show you have understood the context of the question, or links between parts of the question.

5 **Look for your conclusion – aim for 'Plus 1'**

Don't introduce new material in the conclusion, but aim to go beyond a simple recap of what you have already said. Try ending in one of the following ways.

- Use words from the question to show the relevance of your answer.

- Pick up the main point in words and phrases from your introduction, and show how your essay has dealt with this – and links to the question.

- Pick up the definitions you started with. Do you need to modify them? Show how this links to the question.

- Highlight the most important factor, issue, consideration, application you have identified (showing how it answers the question) and **add a comment about it – Plus 1.**

How to work on your plan

1 Jot down points.

2 Outline the body: major sections.

3 Work on the body: plan the structure.

4 Decide on your introduction.

5 Look for your conclusion – aim for 'Plus 1'.

Building a factual essay

Look back to the essay you analysed in Section 3.3.

Account for the emergence of the policy of privatization developed by successive Conservative governments during the 1980s.

Here you had to give (adequate) reasons to explain an event or process, itself tightly defined in context and time. You discovered all this from close analysis of the question. How do you do this through the essay?

In a factual essay,

you have to show that you	you do this
• know your subject in detail	in the **introduction** by • defining and explaining key terms
:the policies of privatization	
• understand the subject	in the **body** by • being **highly selective** about what you put in and what you leave out. You may also have to • analyse information • apply principles to a new context • explain in detail the workings of something
:the emergence of these policies	
	• trace causes or consequences • describe problems and solutions • show similarities between apparently different things, and differences between apparently similar things and much more . . .
• can make sense of the processes you have described.	In the **conclusion** by • drawing conclusions, or extracting general principles from the processes you have described.
:highlight major factor(s) in the emergence of policy.	

Developing Writing-Writing Essays

The division of essay writing tasks into 'factual' and 'judgement' is used in this guide as a planning aid, not because 'judgement' essays do not need evidence or 'factual' essays list the facts. Far from it. The division is useful because

- 'judgement' essays get their structure from the conclusion – a point on the scale between one extreme and the other

- in 'factual' essays you have to work towards your own conclusion and develop a structure along the way. Nevertheless, you can think of this as a blueprint, summarized below.

3.8 How to plan a factual essay: Blueprint 2

1 Analyse the question

How to analyse the question

1 Identify the subject.	Box it.
2 Identify the instruction.	Underline it.
3 Identify the key aspect(s).	Double underline.
4 Look for other significant words that help to pinpoint the scope of your answer.	Use a wiggly line.
5 Ask questions about words and phrases in the question.	
What does this word mean?	
What does this imply?	Scribble, annotate.

What are the reasons for staffing problems within the hotel and catering industry? Suggest ways these might be overcome.

---

2   Plan an outline answer

How to draw an instant plan

1 Take a whole side of A4.

2 Give yourself two minutes.

3 Do several quick sketches.

4 Use only the words and phrases in the question.

5 Show links.

6 Look for a pattern or structure.

What <u>are</u> the <u>reasons</u> for staffing problems within the hotel and catering industry? <u>Suggest</u> ways these might be <u>overcome</u>.

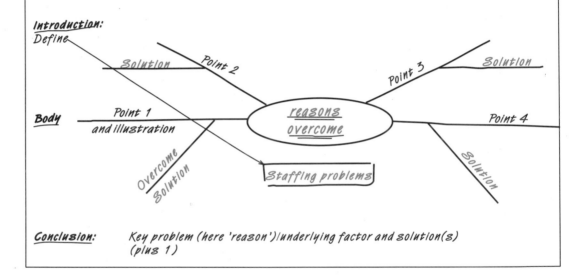

Introduction:
Define

Body

Point 1
and illustration

Solution   *Point 2*

Overcome
Solution

reasons
overcome

Staffing problems

Point 3   *Solution*

Point 4

Solution

Conclusion: *Key problem (here 'reason')/underlying factor and solution(s)*
(plus 1)

3   Work on your plan

How to work on your plan

1 Jot down points.

2 Outline the body: major sections.

3 Work on the body: plan the structure.

4 Decide on your introduction.

5 Look for your conclusion – aim for 'Plus 1'.

Activity

Try this approach to planning another factual essay, taking a title from the list on p. 19.

Have a go at adding some content. It doesn't matter if you don't know anything about the subject – make it up, to get some points in the body.

Developing Writing-Writing Essays

3.2 How to analyse the question: Activity

Be critical. Look at both sides   Only a view. Evidence?

Critically discuss the view that the

define — policy on privatisation promoted by

successive Conservative governments

Several   since 1979 has been a success — define

ie 1979 - 199__

Yes? No?

Arguments for   Arguments against

4   Glimpsing the process

This chapter looks at the process of writing coursework essays. Exam essays are different in purpose and process: you will have been through the learning processes tracked in this chapter earlier in the course. Here you have to perform under pressure of time, for assessment purposes.

Use the diagram on p. 5 to help you decide whether you want to look at this chapter or move straight on to chapter 5 (Writing the essay) after the short section on writing exam essays in section 4.9.

4.1   Uncertainties about writing

Writing is a complex process, and one about which everyone – even experienced writers – feels uniquely anxious. Why is this? And what can you do about it? Here are some thoughts.

Writing – for some reason – is a high-status activity. If you're good at it, you're seen as clever, so if you're not. . . ? Nobody minds saying they're lousy at maths – but lousy at writing? The pressure to succeed is great, and every writer feels it.

> *This is strange, because academic writing is a skill, not a natural talent, so you can get better at it if you work on it, and become rusty if you haven't written for a while. There is no need to feel on the line.*

Writing is a lonely business. Even if you're working 'with' or in the same room as others, you alone have to struggle with thoughts and ideas and get them into words on the page. The first thing to go if you feel isolated is your ability to judge the quality of what you have written. Is it brilliant? Is it rubbish? You can veer uncertainly between the two.

> *Anything you can do to lessen the isolation in which you write is a good idea. Talk through your plans with someone. Ask them to read your first draft and give you specific comments: 'keep this bit', 'add a sentence here to link this with the title', not just nice comments: 'Yeah, this is fine – don't worry'.*

This private writing is posted off for public consumption – and judgement. Praise, when it comes, is very welcome, but nobody likes the feeling of being judged and found wanting.

> *Anything you can do to lessen the feeling of arbitrariness about the assessment process is helpful. Use the suggestions in Chapter 2 for this.*

In short, many of the uncertainties we feel about writing stem from a fear of the unknown. So if you know what is involved in each stage, the fear is taken out of it, and you have a series of practical tasks to undertake. This is why the approach in this guide is to structure the process so you can see the tasks: then you can build the skills.

4.2   Drawing up an action plan

How?

When?

Where?

Your answers to these questions will point you towards an action plan organized around your deadlines. You may like to try some of these suggestions.

Draw a timeline

First, mark in the deadlines. Then put in the stages that need to be completed early in the period before each deadline: browsing (to find useful books and articles); reading (longer sections, short articles); sorting out lecture notes and handouts; planning and carrying out any practical experiences you need to draw on. Finally schedule time to plan and write the first draft of your essay, to review it and to rewrite it for the final presentation.

Activity

List the stages of the essay you are working on. Then draw a timeline, and mark on the points by which you want to have completed each stage.

Week 1   2   3   4   5   6   7   8   9   10
    | | | | | | | | | |

You may find it better to draw your timeline vertically down your page, so your handwriting is horizontal.

Leave a margin of time, because life is never that simple. You will have other deadlines for other courses, job commitments, family commitments. These fixed points need to be marked in too. Then there is the unexpected – flu, a sudden invitation. You need a margin, so you can enjoy – or endure – the unexpected.

List the specifics

Break down the major tasks from the timeline into specifics.

- Draw up a list of things to do. Break it down into do-able tasks: *read two chapters of the key text, find the article on . . .*

- Rejig your list to put first things first.

- Look at your diary.

Plan your week

It is a useful exercise, every now and again, to complete a timetable for a few days, in which you record – truthfully – how you really do spend your time.

Then look at it critically: mark in the genuinely fixed points – family time, work commitments, travel, favourite programmes, seminars, lectures. Then decide how best to use the spaces that are left. Look for

- **start-up** slots: a few minutes to plan your next work sessions

- **working** slots: short slots for specifics, e.g., reading a chapter in a reserved book, finding articles, checking data in reference material; longer slots for practical work, pulling work together, writing. The important point is that working slots do not have to be great long chunks of time. There are not many of them.

- **review** slots: a few minutes to take stock, look back, look ahead – and write lists.

Write TO DO lists

Include everything you have to do today, in small bites, and tick them off when you have done them. Carry over the remaining TO DOs to tomorrow. Watch out for any item you carry over more than three times.

- Is it too big to do in a day? Break it down into smaller chunks.

- Do you feel stressed about it? Break it down and take the first step today. Look at it.

The time you spend thinking and planning – not staring into space – will save you far more time in undirected reading and false starts. However you decide to do it, you must

- think about and analyse your task

- plan to meet the assessment criteria, however expressed

- work to an action plan.

You will then be well prepared for the next steps.

4.3   Gathering material

You will have to go and look for and generate your material. Try the following.

- What do you know already? Your analysis of the question and outline plan will probably have shown you that you do know quite a bit about the subject. Pinpoint what you need to find out.

- What are you expected to know? Your lecture handouts, notes, and course outlines will give you the bottom line. If you understand them, you know them. If you don't, do some specific research to find out the points about which you are unclear.

- Do the basic reading – the relevant chapters from a core text.

- Extend your reading: follow up one or two references to books on a particular aspect of your topic, and look at some articles to bring you up to date.

Do you read economically?

Survey the text critically: take in the title, subtitle, blurb, author, date of publication. Use the contents and index to locate information speedily.

Question the text. What information/interpretation do you want from the text? Are you getting your answers?

Read effectively

Skim some bits for an overview. Find the summaries (beginning or end of chapters?) and read them first. Read the first sentence of a paragraph before you decide to read it all.

Scan if you are looking for a particular piece of information or reference. Ignore everything except what you are looking for.

Read in detail only when you have to! Keep yourself awake by

- **recalling** the main points of what you've read at the end of each section.

- **making notes.** Go for the main points and supporting evidence relevant to your purpose – not necessarily the same main points as the author presents them. Don't copy except for short phrases you may want as quotes.

- **reviewing** your notes, and checking quickly with the original to make sure you have not missed anything crucial.

Try it. This should cut down on the time you spend reading, not increase it.

Record your sources

List all your sources meticulously, so you know where ideas or studies come from. If you don't, you may

- have to retrace your steps later – which is very annoying and time consuming

- not get the credit for the work you have done

- not realize that you are plagiarizing, by using other people's ideas without acknowledging them.

For an accurate bibliography, you need the seven points of information (where applicable) in the illustration below. If you get into the habit of recording details in this

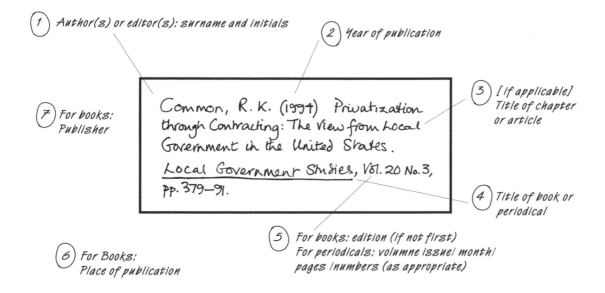

order, you will find your bibliography is virtually written.

Other examples are given in Student Guide 1: *Essential Writing Skills*, Chapter 9.

4.4 Distilling ideas: getting something on paper

This is where you flick through your mounting pile of paper and then put it to one side.

- Jot down thoughts and points as they come to you.
- Note the studies, commentators, case studies that prompted these thoughts.
- Link theory with practice (your own experiences or studies).
- Have more points and thoughts than you can use.
- Distinguish between your researches (your knowledge base, including commentators and interpretations) and your opinions (what you think about what you found out).

4.5 Planning your essay

Look again at the question, and your outline plan. For a judgement essay, look back to **How to work on your plan**, Section 3.5. Have your initial views changed? Or are they reinforced? Check your position on the sliding scale, and work backwards through the body to note the material that seems strong to you. Then move on to linking in the other points and ideas you have noted.

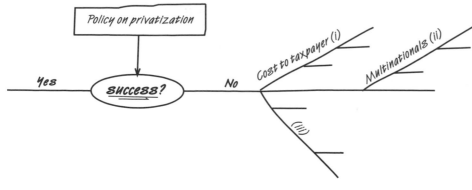

In Essay 2 on the privatization policies, you can add arguments and evidence to the outline plan. Show each argument as a main heading: link the evidence to it.

For a factual essay, look back to **How to work on your plan, Section 3.7.** Can you refine your definitions? Do any factors/measures/features now stand out? These points may give you a strong introduction and conclusion. Then add your points to make your case/detail your study.

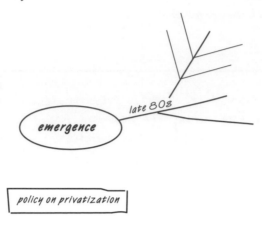

In Essay 1, you can add points and illustration to the outline plan. Show each **point** as a main heading: link the **illustration** or evidence to it.

By the time you have finished working on your plan, you should be able to see the parts of your essay clearly.

The structure of an essay	
Your essay will have	**in which you**
• an **introduction** (one paragraph or 1/10th of your essay)	• explain how you interpret the question, define key terms, show the limits of your essay
• a **body** (the bulk of your essay)	• show that you know the key issues/factors/processes/ interpretations, and can support these points with evidence
	• understand the importance and have a view about these key issues (in a judgement essay)
	• select the key points and use them in the way asked for (in a factual essay)
• a **conclusion** (one paragraph or 1/10th of your essay)	• show where you stand in the debate (judgement)
	• can draw conclusions or extract general principles (factual).

4.6   Writing the first draft

In coursework essays you can make two drafts, so you don't have to worry about what you first efforts look like. Approach the writing of a coursework essay in any way that gets you going. Different ways work for different people.

- Just write fast, uncorrected, in any order. Work on the structure later.

- Use a pencil. Use a biro. Use a word processor. Use whatever helps you get the first few lines down.

- Think about a particular reader. Write for them.

- Write different bits on separate sheets, so you can shuffle the order later.

- Don't worry about the fiddly bits. Keep your momentum going.

Or just start! Begin at the beginning and work straight through. This may be less difficult than you think if you've followed the steps in this guide.

4.7   Reviewing and editing your essay

Don't skip this. If you need convincing, look at the introductions and conclusions in sections 5.2 and 5.7.

Review your essay for structure

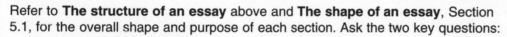

> **Activity**
>
> Go back to the assessment criteria you have been given, and check that your essay meets the criteria on structure. Make changes to ensure it does. These will probably be quite minor – adding a linking or topic sentence, at most moving a paragraph.
>
> Refer to **The structure of an essay** above and **The shape of an essay**, Section 5.1, for the overall shape and purpose of each section. Ask the two key questions:
>
> • does it 'answer the question'?
>
> • is it 'well structured'?

Edit your essay for avoidable errors

Errors in spelling, punctuation, quotations, citations, typograhpical erors (?) – you can (and must) eliminate these at this point. Don't just rely on a spell check: read the conclusions in Section 5.7 if you need convincing.

4.8   Writing the final draft

With two drafts you gain

- fluency: you are not inhibited by having to edit as you go

- accuracy: you can act on the faults you spotted in your reviewing and editing

- objectivity: you can distance yourself from the content and look at it from your reader's perspective

- good presentation: you separate the writing and thinking from the editing and presentation.

Writing two drafts may even save time.

The processes of reviewing, editing and redrafting will run together if you use a word processor. This is great in some ways – you can move bits around and tweak this and that – but there comes a point when you must decide that this is the best you can manage – and stop!

4.9 Writing exam essays

Exam essays are different: the process is streamlined, the purpose clear-cut – assessment – and the key constraint is time. Your whole approach to essay writing is driven by this constraint.

Budgeting time

1 An overall time budget

How do you allocate time in a 'three questions in three hours' exam? Simple arithmetic suggests one hour each, but if you allow a full hour for your first question, you are bound to be short. Why?

From the overall three hours, you need to deduct time to

- read the paper and finalize your choice of question: five to ten minutes

- check your script at the end: another ten minutes.

This leaves you with 50/55 minutes per question. You can reduce time on one question a little if you really don't know enough to answer it, and redeploy the surplus, but don't be tempted to spend longer on one just because you do know a lot about it. You'll end up writing an all-I-know-about-it answer, AND having to skimp on the rest.

2 A marks-per-minute budget

Allocate time between questions according to the marks the questions attract. Look at the shape of past exam papers and do the basic arithmetic on marks per minute well in advance – keeping an eye out for the unexpected. Once you have done your sums, stick to your time allocation in the exam.

3 A time-within-question budget

Within the time you have allocated for each question, allow time for each part of the writing process, or, in short answers, each part of the question. In the 55 minutes allowed for each essay in a three-essays-in-three-hours paper, allow time to

- analyse and plan your answer (five to ten minutes)

- review and edit (five minutes)

- write the essay (45 minutes).

Activity

Work out a detailed time budget for each of the exam papers below, using the points made under the three time budget headings above.

Paper 1

Time: Three hours

Instruction: Answer QUESTION 1 and TWO OTHER questions.

All questions carry equal marks.

The questions:

1   (Compulsory question)

Define and write brief notes on FIVE of the following:

(a ——h)

2 – 8   Essay questions

Paper 2

Time: Two hours

Instruction: Answer TWO questions, ONE from SECTION A and ONE

from SECTION B. All questions carry equal marks.

The questions:

Section A : Essay questions 1 – 4

Section B : Essay questions 5 – 8

Paper 3

Time: Two hours

Instruction: Students must answer THREE questions.

Answer the question in SECTION A and TWO

QUESTIONS from SECTION B.

The questions:

Section A is worth 50% of the total marks

available in the examination.

Each (essay) question in Section B is worth 25%

of the total marks available.

Whatever the context in which you are writing, your aim when you write an essay is to produce a piece of work that

- answers the question (your reader's purpose)

- meets the assessment criteria (your purpose)

- pleases you and your reader, both in its appearance and in the clarity and organization of its content.

5 Writing the essay

This chapter looks at the practicalities of turning an essay plan into an essay. The target, as ever, is to focus on detail so that the essay pleases everyone:

- your reader – by answering the question
- you – by meeting the assessment criteria.

5.1 The shape of an essay

How do you see your essay?

As a swimming pool?

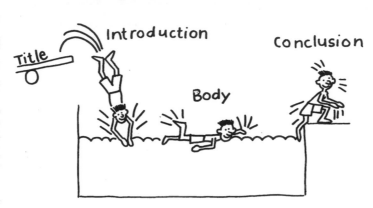

a maze?

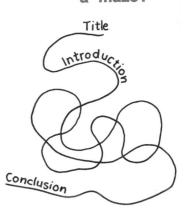

a crochet loop?

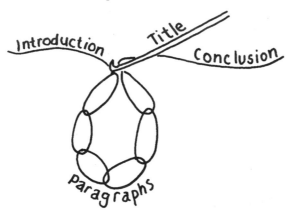

a journey?

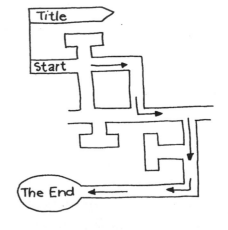

a series of crunch points?

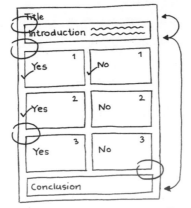

a racetrack?

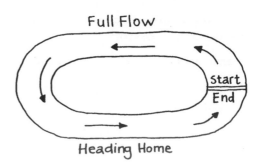

Developing Writing-Writing Essays

Whatever image you have of your essay, and the process of writing it, one thing is clear – that, like any other process, every essay has a beginning, a middle and an end:

- an introduction
- a body
- a conclusion.

Each of these has a particular purpose and structure, and particular crunch points you need to focus on as you plan and write. The diagram below shows the crunch points we focus on in this chapter.

TITLE: WRITING THE ESSAY

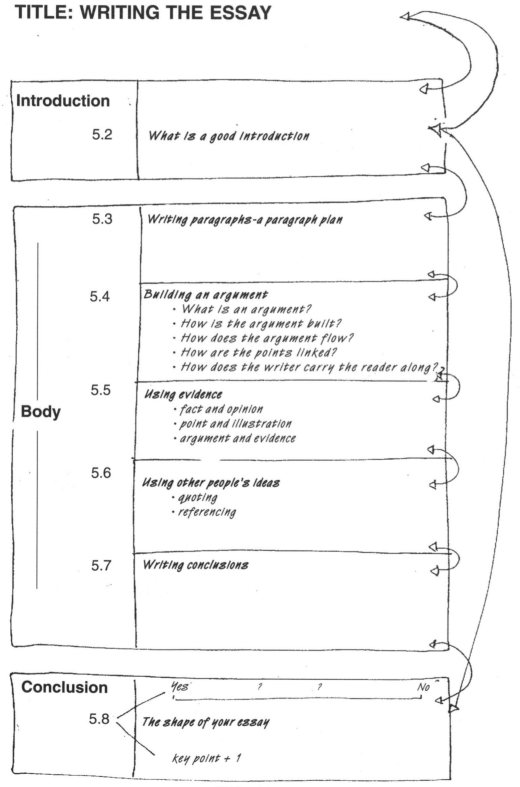

Introduction

5.2   *What is a good introduction*

Body

5.3   *Writing paragraphs–a paragraph plan*

5.4   *Building an argument*
- *What is an argument?*
- *How is the argument built?*
- *How does the argument flow?*
- *How are the points linked?*
- *How does the writer carry the reader along?*

5.5   *Using evidence*
- *fact and opinion*
- *point and illustration*
- *argument and evidence*

5.6   *Using other people's ideas*
- *quoting*
- *referencing*

5.7   *Writing conclusions*

Conclusion

   Yes   *?*   *?*   *No*

5.8   *The shape of your essay*

     key point + 1

5.2 Writing introductions

How much can you tell about an essay from the introduction? The answer, as any tutor or examiner will tell you, is 'a lot'. By the end of this section, I hope you will see why.

The section is practical: the activity comes first and the points about writing introductions follow.

Extract 1

The success of Hotel and Catering operations depends on manpower. Trained and qualified staff are therefore essential for the adequate running of an establishment or failure is inevitable. Within the hotel and Catering industry there is a multiplicity of different types and sizes of organisation. The hotel and catering industry is considered labour intensive.

Extract 2

The hotel and catering industry has had a notorious reputation for high labour turnover and its problems of attracting the right people, even when unemployement is running at very high levels. In recent years however, turnover in some sectors has reduced dramatically, probably as a result of several different factors such as high unemployment, improving induction and training methods and the unfair dismissals legislation.

Developing Writing-Writing Essays

Extract 3

The Hotel and Catering industry can often be a very stressful and soul-destroying industry to work in. It can affect everybody who works in this industry from the cleaners and chambermaids up to the hotel or restaurant manager, for example. It is by no means a '9 to 5' office job, and the staff involved in this industry must be prepared to be flexible with the hours they work. Because this industry is so stressful, it is important that there is a good manager or supervisor and that teamwork is displayed. However, this is not always the case in the Hotel and Catering industry which can create many difficulties throughout the workforce. Having said that there are staffing problems, this does not mean that the Hotel and Catering industry is doomed, there are ways in which these problems can be diluted or even overcome.

Extract 4

As is the case with all industries the Hotel and Catering Industry is a great contributor to Gross National Product. Being in the top five industries means that it contributes higher than average amounts. Unlike most industries Hotel and Catering relies heavily upon Tourism from abroad. So even if there is a recession in a particular country there will still be a certain amount of income, through visitors from abroad. As travel become both cheaper and easier tourists will come from further afield, so will increase overall. In 1989, the year that the British Tourist Authority was established there were 5 million overseas visitors, to Britain. By 1992 this figure had risen to 18.5 million. By the end of 1993 it is forecast that foreign visitors will have spent £24 billion in the UK, thus helping pay foreign debt payments, but also increasing foreign currency reserves.

Extract 5

During a time of recession and high unemployment it seems hard to believe that, "two million new recruits will be needed by the hotel and catering industry in the next three years to counter skill shortages and staff losses". (Afiya 1992). However, this is one of the main staffing problems facing the industry today. Reasons contributing to this problem include the "substantial growth in the demand for staff as the industry comes out of recession" (Afiya 1992), the poor image of the industry, low pay, long and antisocial hours and lack of , or inadequate training. This essay goes on to analyse these reasons in further detail and to suggest ways in which they can be overcome.

> The Hotel and Catering industry is considered to be one of the biggest employers in Britain. There are over 2 million people employed in the tourist industry, more than half of them are employed in the hotel and catering sector. It is probably one of the most active sectors in the industry in terms of creating new jobs. It has demonstrated its resilience in times of economic recession and its ability to recover more quickly than many other tourism-related activities. However, there are a number of problems which are related to this sector in terms of employment and labour. In this essay I shall try to locate these problems and discuss the ways in which they could be resolved.

When you have finished, compare your grading and comments with other people's and discuss the reasons for agreement and differences. Then, before you read on, compare your comments with mine at the end of the chapter.

You probably found it easier to mark these introductions than you thought, because as reader/assessor you had one overriding criterion:

'Is this essay going to answer the question?'

This is the key criterion for any essay. Most of the assessment criteria in Chapter 2 relate to structure and relevance: now you see why. Everything in an essay has to work towards this key purpose.

In brief

In an introduction you must show

- that you are going to answer the question
- how you will set about answering the question.

You do this by

- using the words and phrases of the question
- showing you know what issues these imply
- indicating the main areas of your discussion in the essay
- making sure everything is relevant, and linked explicitly to the question.

Specifically,

- make a clear statement of the main point in the first or second sentence (a 'topic sentence'; see below)
- show enough of your plan of the essay to let your reader see that you are in control and to the point (four or five sentences)
- have a purposeful style – no waffle
- indicate that you will have evidence for the points you put forward
- end with a sentence that links back to the topic sentence, and to the title.

5.3 Writing paragraphs

In the introductions above you were looking for a paragraph with a highly specific purpose. Here we look at the basic structure and purpose of a paragraph.

Paragraphs have a structure.

- A paragraph is a short block of text that develops **one main idea.**

- This main idea is usually expressed clearly in one sentence – the **topic sentence.**

- The topic sentence is usually the **first** in the paragraph.

- Paragraphs have a internal **structure:** a beginning, a middle and an end.

This structure has a purpose: to make it easier

- to **read:** you know where to look for the main idea, and can see how each one is developed.

- to **plan:** each paragraph develops a single main point. You can link related points and plan the overall structure.

- to **write:** new point, new paragraph. Start each paragraph with a clear statement of the point you are making, then add detail.

How to write paragraphs

All you need to start your paragraph is an idea – a main point you want to put across. The rest is straightforward when you work to a plan.

A paragraph plan

1 **Start with the topic sentence**
   - to express the main idea.

2 **Explain or define** any abstract or problematic terms
   - to clarify the topic sentence.

3 **Show your evidence**
   - to support your main idea or argument in the topic sentence.

4 **Comment on the evidence**
   - to show how it supports or develops the main idea.
     If appropriate, mention other evidence (examples/studies/experiments/interpretations) to widen the discussion.

5 **Conclude**
   - to explain consequences or implications
   - to show the development of the argument
   - to link back to the idea in the topic sentence
   - to link forward to the main idea in the next paragraph
   - (in the first and last paragraphs of an essay or section) to show the link with the title or section heading.

Activity

Try it. Below is a paragraph from a student's answer to the same essay question:

What are the reasons for staffing problems within the hotel and catering industry? Suggest ways in which these might be overcome.

How does it match the structure of the paragraph plan?

1 What is the main idea? Where is this expressed most clearly?

2 What is the function of each sentence in the paragraph?

3 Does it end well?

```
The career image of the hospitality industry is poor. Firstly, it
is perceived as having low rates of pay, which contributes to
the poor image of the industry. This means that the industry is
at a disadvantage in attracting and retaining good staff. In a
report entitled 'Tomorrow's Workforce', published by the Hotel
and Catering Training Company (HCTC), results of a survey showed
that 'jobs in the industry are commonly rated by students as
having lower status than jobs requiring similar skills and
qualifications in other industries'. The industry seems to be
doing little to combat this perception. The survey also showed
that careers information available to students and young people
making decisions about their future careers was inadequate and of
poor quality.
```

Do your analysis and then check your comments with mine in the feedback section.

Activity

Try writing a paragraph of your own following this profile. The numbers below correspond to those in the paragraph plan.

1 Write down the main idea as clearly and simply as you can: this is your topic sentence.

2 Write one sentence to explain or define.

3 Write one sentence to show your evidence.

4 Write one sentence in which you comment on the evidence.

5 Write one sentence to conclude – to show how you have developed the idea in the topic sentence.

In all, you should have a paragraph of five sentences.

Alternatively, you could work from the topic sentence of the next paragraph in the student's essay above:

```
As the recession comes to an end, not only will the industry
require extra staff, but increased training and education will
be needed too.
```

Further examples of paragraphs to consider and work on are given in
Student Guide 1: *Essential Writing Skills*, Chapter 7.

How long is a paragraph?

How long is a piece of string? Long enough to do what you want it to? Or not? The same applies to paragraphs. A principle: a paragraph needs to be long enough to develop an idea in the way outlined in the paragraph plan.

Some guidelines:

- In academic writing, one sentence is not a paragraph. You cannot develop an idea in one sentence. The same applies to two, and often to three.

- If you have more than ten sentences, or three-quarters of a side of writing, you have probably failed to spot when you moved on to a new point: new point, new paragraph.

- Five to eight sentences is a good guideline. These may be short or long, and will give you enough flexibility to develop your ideas along the lines of the paragraph plan.

The best way to get a feel for the length of paragraphs is to read critically – bearing in mind that, in writing an essay, you are engaging in a specialist form of academic writing. Most of the other forms of writing you see around you will be working to different conventions: textbooks tend to have long and detailed paragraphs; articles in learned journals are often even longer, possibly because the authors are less experienced as writers. Some periodicals you read have a different primary market – busy practitioners – in which case their sentences and paragraphs will be shorter. Then, of course, there is coffee-time reading: tabloid journalists go for the one-shot punch – and the one-sentence paragraph.

The model for paragraphs in essays is other essays. These can be hard to get hold of, because essay writing is private form of writing . . . as we saw in Chapter 4. So keep your eyes out for examples of successful essay writing, and see how the functions of a paragraph plan can be carried out in shorter and longer blocks of text . . . starting with the extract in Section 5.4 below.

5.4   Building an argument

Each paragraph is a microcosm of your essay, a building block with its own place, wedged between the one before and the one after. Your task as a writer is to make each one actively carry out your purpose: build your argument, trace consequences, make a case or whatever.

- **Start each paragraph with a topic sentence linking your point to the title.**

- **End each paragraph it by showing how you have developed your point.**

This section takes the form of an extended activity. We will be looking at some of the many ways in which you can use the structure of paragraphs to build an argument. The material for this section is an extract from a student's term paper.

The dominance of the West on the world economy and its relationship with third world underdevelopment.

THE AID SYNDROME

Aid is presented, on the whole, as open-handed charity, yet the reality is somewhat different. A great deal of aid is conditional on certain projects being carried out. Many of these projects are commissioned, developed and implemented by the personnel of developed countries. These projects benefit private companies in the donor countries in terms of revenue and employment and often involve minimal transfer of expertise. Plant or infrastructure is installed by Western contractors and indigenous people provide labour and maintenance.

This kind of aid can be counter-productive; it reinforces patterns of dependence, sapping self-esteem and national will to find local solutions to local problems using local resources, labour and 'appropriate' scale technology. The surplus funds available in the West to supply this aid are also part of the underdevelopment problem. Despite our massive dependence on the resources of the third world, we do not pay fair enough prices for these nations to be able to accrue enough capital themselves to fund these major projects. At times it appears almost as if, for some countries, the colonial system has not ended, merely been spatially displaced to new headquarters at the World Bank, the IMF and the business capitals of the West.

The well-known adage on this cycle of continuing domination and dependence is that the third world needs fishing rods, not fish. This is part of the answer but belies the continuing inability of many Westerners to break out of the patronization of colonial consciousness. What is really needed is locally produced fishing rods and a fair price for them and the fish they catch, should there be sufficient surplus to export.

Reproduced with thanks to Paul O'Carroll.

1   What is the argument?

Where do you look for it? The clearest statements should be in the first and last sentences:

- the topic sentence of the first paragraph for a statement of the argument

- the concluding sentence of the last to show the view the writer has worked towards.

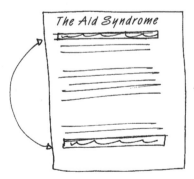

Try it.
Read the first and last sentences.

2 How is the argument built?

Look now for the structure of each paragraph. Check each one against the paragraph plan.

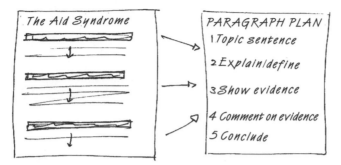

You will find a clear statement of the main idea in the topic sentence of each paragraph, and a tight structure to the development of the idea.

3 How does the argument flow?

Here you need to look at the last sentence of each paragraph.

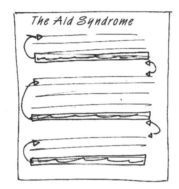

Look at how it has developed from the point in the topic sentence.
Look at how it links with and leads to the topic sentence of the next paragraph.

4 How are the points linked?

Look at how each paragraph develops from the argument and explanations in the previous paragraph. Look closely at what words like 'these', 'this' refer to: *these projects, this kind of aid, this cycle.*

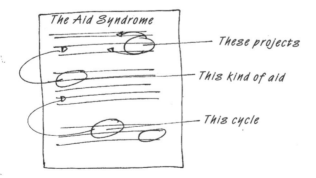

This piece has a logical construction. As readers, we are not asked to grasp a conclusion before we have a good grasp of the issues. With this understanding, and drawn along by the writer's argument, we are led into the next part of the argument.

5 How does the writer carry the reader along?

You can see, at each level of construction we have considered so far, how this writer carries the reader along. This works at the micro-level of sentence construction too. He makes discreet use of words that carry the argument along: the surplus funds are *also* part of . . .; at times it appears *almost as if* . . .; and words that signal a change in direction: *yet* the reality is some what different . . .; this is part of the answer *but* . . .

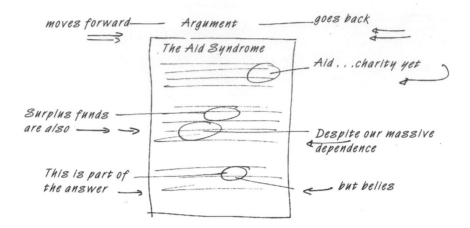

Other words often used to signal another point that moves the argument forward are: *moreover; not only . . . but also; for example*. Words that signal that a contrasting idea is about to be put forward include: *however; on the other hand; whereas; nevertheless*.

This student has been skilful in this essay in his use of structure and language, so that, as readers, we are unaware of it, and simply accept the case he makes. This is effective writing. Only when you analyse it do you see the skill with which it is put together – and how important structure is in any piece of writing

- at the macro-level of overall construction – of the essay, the section, within and between paragraphs

- at the micro-level of the use of language in argument.

How long is a paragraph (again)?

> ## Activity
>
> Count the sentences in each of the paragraphs in the extract from 'The Aid Syndrome'.
>
> Analyse each paragraph to see if and how it follows the pattern of the paragraph plan.
>
> What does this add to your sense of how long a paragraph should be?

5.5 Using evidence

You know the difference between **fact** and **opinion**:

FACT

OPINION

Shares in the following publicly
owned utilities were floated on
the Stock Market:

BP . . . BT . . . BWater . . . BR . . .

Privatization? Daylight robbery
of the taxpayer . . .

Privatization? Brilliant – they're
round like greased lightening . . .

Your task in academic writing is to draw on both to build an argument. You can use fact as illustration to support your point:

POINT
+
ILLUSTRATION

Privatization has strengthened the hand of the consumer
by stressing the role of the public as consumers or customers.
BP . . . BT . . . BWater . . . BR . . . 'passengers' = 'customers' . . .

More often in academic writing you are not in a position to check 'the facts'; you are dealing with the ideas and interpretations of other practitioners and writers in your field. These sources then become the evidence on which you draw to support your argument.

ARGUMENT
+
EVIDENCE

Privatization has produced a spate of Citizen's Charters,
although whether this has strengthened the hand of the
consumer is debatable. Bloggs (1992), in her study of flood
victims, reported a higher level of . . . Snookes (1993) raised
additional questions about . . .

Activity

Each of the statements below is the topic sentence of a paragraph in a student's essay. Read each one, and jot down your reactions as a reader.

1 Social class is unbalanced in inner-city areas, with a disproportionately high number of unskilled groups . . .

2 It is obvious that green belts have played a very important role in planning. Without them, urban sprawl would most definitely have occurred . . .

3 Exhaustive social science and nursing research has been done in this area, resulting in a more holistic view of the variables involved . . .

As a reader, your reactions may include

• Surprise: really? *Let's see this exhaustive research.*

• Hostility: who says? *Have you ever set foot in a city?*

• Irritation: *obvious? Who to? You? Me? Show me/persuade me – don't tell me/lecture me.*

Tutors' comments are more restrained:

- *What's your basis or evidence for saying this?*

- *Argue by evidence or deduction, not assertion.*

- *Is it? Can you prove this? Avoid such argument by assertion.*

• EVIDENCE????

Showing the evidence for your assertions is an aspect of courteousness to your reader. No one likes to be talked at – handed down opinions they cannot challenge – especially when these are disguised as facts. So don't make

- sweeping generalizations

- unsupported assertions – which are really no more than opinions.

5.6 Using other people's ideas

Other people's ideas about your subject is, in large part, what academic study is about. This is more the case in disciplines where interpretation of texts and events is the subject matter itself – as in aspects of psychology, history, literature – and less so in subjects where problem-solving and experimentation are central activities. Nevertheless, in all subjects you need to recognize where your direct experience of a subject ends and the interpretations and experiences of others begin.

You have to be clear about who did what, and who said what. You show this by referencing and quoting accurately. This section gives a brief outline of the processes involved when you do this. For more detailed guidance, see Student Guide 1: *Essential Writing Skills,* Chapter 9.

Activity

Read the extracts below from students' essays and the comments on them.
Key points about quoting and using references follow.

Extract 1

> We have dealt here with many of the historical, structural and continuing socio-economic factors which have contributed to underdevelopment in the third world and in many cases are still doing so. None of these alone is sufficient to explain the massive underachievement of the tropical nations despite the enormous vitality of its resources and vitality of its people. According to Schumacher (1974), it is the underlying global economic status quo which explains the persistence of all the factors . . .

Comment: The brief mention in the text (author and date) keeps the ideas moving. Full details will be found in the bibliography arranged in alphabetical order at the end of the essay:

Schumacher, E. F. (1973) *Small is Beautiful*. London, Blond and Briggs.

Extract 2

Nursing science involves a knowledge base whose material is drawn from both the physical sciences and social sciences (Chalmers 1986). The idea, however, that there is an art to nursing is essential to our understanding of the nursing process. The art of nursing has been described as 'that intuitive act' (Robinson and Vaughan 1992) which enables a nurse to respond to the unexpected. Nursing is a practice discipline in which each situation that presents itself to the nurse is unique, yet the nurse must be equipped to make clinical decisions appropriate to each event:

nursing, as a practice discipline, draws on this knowledge in specific practice situations which are all intrinsically unique (Robinson and Vaughan 1992, p. 170).

The implications of this are that . . .

Comment: In this extract the student makes two references. The full references in the bibliography are

Chalmers, H. (1990) Nursing Models and the Relationship to the Nursing Process and Nursing Theory. In: Salvage, J. and Kershaw, B. (ed.) *Models for Nursing*. London, Scutari, pp. 29–37.

Robinson, K. and Vaughan, B. (1992) *Knowledge for Nursing Practice*. Oxford, Butterworth Heinemann.

The writer also has two quotations, one short, incorporated into the flow of the text; one long, indented. Of the two, the long quotation is of more dubious value. You only need a quotation when you want to discuss the precise wording – not to prove that you have read to book! Make sure you comment on the words you quote.

Check the method of referencing preferred in your department. The examples here are cited in the Harvard (or 'author-date') system. The British Standard System contains all the same elements, but with the date at the end. The link with the text is made by a number immediately after the author's name.

The reference in the first extract would appear as follows:

in the text: According to Schumacher [6], it is the underlying global economic status quo . . .

in the bibliography: (6) Schumacher, E.F. *Small is Beautiful*. London, Blond and Briggs, 1973.

In brief

Quote when it is important to use and comment on the precise wording of another writer.

• Run a **short quote** into your text.

• Indent a **long quote**.

Reference other people's ideas or research when you draw on them.

In your **bibliography**, list all the books, articles, periodicals and other sources you have consulted.

You can see why it is important to keep an accurate record of your sources as you go along. Check back to Section 4.3 for a reminder of the points you need to record.

5.7 Writing conclusions

How much can you tell about an essay from the conclusion? The answer, as any tutor or examiner will tell you, is 'a lot'. By the end of this section, I hope you will see why.

This is the same wording as the lead-in to the activity on reading and assessing introductions because the issues are much the same: first impressions/last impressions. The question **'Is this essay going to answer the question?'** becomes **'Has this essay answered the question?'**

Activity: What is a good conclusion?

Below are the six conclusions to the same essay, in the same order as the introductions. Your task, as a tutor or examiner in a hurry, is

1   to grade them, as they stand, noting your reasons

2   to grade the essay as a whole, based on your reading of the introductions and conclusions only.

What are the reasons for staffing problems within the hotel and catering industry? Suggest ways in which these might be overcome.

Extract 1

> Poor pay with unsociable hours may be a dominant factor for staffing problems, Managerial positions are both demanding on skill and flexibility, but with more training, revised employment contracts and better working conditions in the Hotel and Catering Industry may not neccesarily be overcome but reduced.

Extract 2

> The results of the study have been positive. Staff turnover has been reduced by a third. Two thirds of our people have worked with us for over two years, 40% for over four years. Profit margins have increased by 17% this shows how that by looking at staff problems and investing money and time in motivating your staff you are able to reap the benefits which are good moral amongst staff members, who obtain a high level of job satisfaction which intern benefits the customer and finally the company financially.

Developing Writing-Writing Essays

There is no denying that there are staffing problems within the Hotel and Catering industry and it would not be true to say that these problems are easily overcome, especially if the industry does not have the finance it needs to solve the problems.

The main pressure for staffing problems are lack of money which links up with bad management and lack of training. Bad management can create many more problems such as lack of motivation, low morale and conflicts in the workplace. In any industry, lack of finance is the beginning of a vicious circle because if there is a lack of finance then this means that the industry has to cut back on certain areas, such as training the workforce which in itself can cause all sorts of major and minor problems. However, good management is essential to running an efficient workforce because of the human relation skills the manager would have and pass onto his workforce. Good management and training are the two most essential ingredients for overcoming staffing problems.

Managers have to make more of an effort to look after their staff. Pay and benefits have to be more competitive, with compensation for bad unsocial hours and a concerted effort to improve both training and working conditions. The staff will then be able to transform better training and conditions into better service for the customer.

The reasons for staffing problems within the hotel and catering industry are varied, but ultimately it is up to the industry to make itself a more attractive employer. A combination of the approaches outlined before will be necessary, but they represent no quick answer, and the labour supply issue will remain a crucial challenge for the industry for the forseeable future.

> Overall I feel the hotel and catering industry is probably one of the best industries available at the moment, because it is very demanding and offers good prospective for the future. The pay may not be as good as others, but it is certainly worthwhile.

When you have finished, compare your grading and comments with other people's and discuss the reasons for agreement and differences. Then compare your comments with mine at the end of the chapter.

5.8 The shape of your essay

When you look back on an essay, can you see the structure? Try some of the images at the start of this chapter if this helps. You should be able to see how

- the end is different to the beginning (the swim)

- the essay has a direction (the journey)

- the question runs like a thread through the essay (the maze)

- each part of the essay is a different phase (the race)

- each paragraph grows from the one before and links to the one that follows, the last linking back to the first (the crochet).

Finally, I hope you can see that this chapter has a structure (the crunch points) that tracks the process you go through when you write your essays.

5.9 Using feedback

Eureka! You've handed your essay in . . . out of sight, out of mind . . . until it comes back with a grade, a mark, an assessment. At this point you become aware, if you were not already, that this essay really does have a reader, that you really did have a purpose in writing. Before you saw it from your perspective; now you have to see it from your tutor's. It is not an easy transition to make.

Why do tutors make comments like these?

'This essay is clearly structured but not effectively enough to answer the question.'

'Good, but make sure subheadings actually reflect content.'

'The content was very superficial.'

'Much of what you say could be relevant, but you leave the reader to infer the relevance, rather than make the connection yourself.'

Tutors give feedback for two reasons:

- to explain or justify a mark: looking backwards, the assessment purpose ('summative' assessment in the jargon)

- to point you to things to change next time you write: looking forwards, the teaching purpose (or 'formative' assessment).

How do you react to comments like these? You, on the receiving end, may not be too pleased with a lengthy analysis of what you did wrong. All you want to know is the mark. However, this is often all the feedback you are going to get, so do use it. Here are some suggestions.

- Read the comments. Many people don't: out of sight, out of mind.

- Think about them. What does 'superficial' mean? That you have not read enough? Or not thought enough about what you have read? Or not developed your paragraphs sufficiently to explain, develop, or illustrate an idea and link it to the title?

- Act on the comments. Do things differently next time.

Use feedback from tutors, whether intended as formative or summative assessment, to move you on in setting your own learning agenda next time you tackle an essay. Feel good about what you've got right (whether or not this attracted comment), and pinpoint what you need to work on.

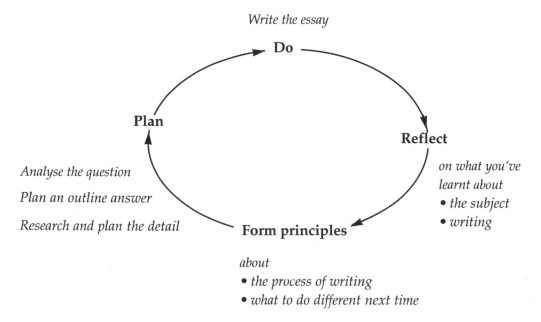

Next time, perhaps you will plan in a slightly different way, will be better prepared for writing, will reflect and extract principles for the next time, and the next . . .

This is the **learning cycle,** at the heart of the essay writing process, as you saw on p. 5 of this guide.

5.10 Self- and peer assessment

You may be asked to make this process more explicit and visible, both to yourself and to your tutor, by including your own assessment of your work ('self-assessment'), or by using feedback from other students ('peer assessment'), as part of the process of writing.

Self-assessment

You may be asked to attach some comments on your work on a sheet, under headings such as these:

- strengths of this essay

- how this essay could be improved

- the grade it deserves

- I'd like your comments on . . .

You may also be asked to comment on how you set about the task – your reading, your attendance at seminars or whatever. You may feel exposed making these assessments of your work, but take it seriously and be realistic, because

- when you stand back from your work, you see it from your reader's perspective. You can then make changes.

- your tutors can see if your perceptions are on track. If your perceptions are very different, higher or lower, it opens up a dialogue about what your – and their – expectations are.

Peer assessment

Whether or not it is a formal part of the system, it is a good idea to ask other people for their impressions of your work early in the process so that you can make changes. If it is a formal system you may be asked to

- get detailed feedback from another student on the first draft of an essay

- keep a record of your reader's comments and the changes you then made.

The idea behind this is to encourage critical thinking – and to produce better writing.

5.11   Feedback on activities in Chapter 5

5.2: What is a good introduction? Activity

What are the reasons for staffing problems within the hotel and catering industry? Suggest ways in which these might be overcome.

1   The first two sentences, although rather obvious, look as if this student is heading towards answering the question. Then the introduction nosedives: instead of indicating that the writer will be discussing 'reasons', there are two irrelevant and unconnected comments about *types of organization* and *labour intensive*. The spelling mistake gives a bad impression.
Verdict: it does not look as if this essay will answer the question – low grade.

2   Two sentences is not a paragraph! You cannot develop ideas enough in two sentences. The phrase 'notorious reputation' looks interesting, and some attempt is made to identify the problems (*turnover of staff* and *attracting the right people*) but this student never ties the points in with the question. The question is about *reasons* (none hinted at) and *suggestions* (surely not *high unemployment?*).
Verdict: no indication that this student will answer the question – low grade.

3   Too long! You can tell that at a glance. The lively start is refreshing – first-hand experience is useful if it brings depth to an issue – but it soon begins to look as if this student is going to wander off the point. Detailed discussion – *flexible . . ., managers/framework* – is for the body. However, this student pulls back to the question at the end. Hooray!
Verdict: likely to be waffly and anecdotal, but it may throw up some good points on the way. If it sticks to the question, a (low) average grade.

4   *GNP, tourism, £27 billion* – all completely irrelevant to the question, which is a pity, because the writer seems well informed – on tourism anyway, if not the hotel and catering industry. These 'facts' are all completely unreferenced – a side issue to the total irrelevance of the material.
Verdict: sorry, mate! Wrong answer to wrong question – I can't see how I can give any marks for this.

Developing Writing-Writing Essays

5   The first sentence catches the attention (yes, it does seem hard to believe) and the rest of the introduction keeps it. A quick taste of what's to come (low pay, long unsocial hours, etc.) tells us that the writer is in control, will answer the question, and has done some reading (although two quotations from the same source are not necessary – one reference would do fine).
Verdict: looks good. High grade.

6   This reads a little stiffly, with a repetitive sentence structure. However, although it is has a rather general approach to *problems*, it shows a serious intention to answer the question.
Verdict: a competent essay.

5.3: Writing paragraphs: Activity

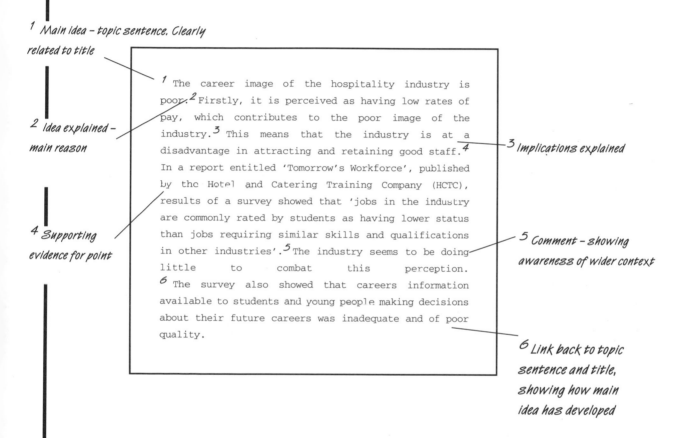

1 *Main idea – topic sentence. Clearly related to title*

2 *Idea explained – main reason*

4 *Supporting evidence for point*

¹ The career image of the hospitality industry is poor. ² Firstly, it is perceived as having low rates of pay, which contributes to the poor image of the industry. ³ This means that the industry is at a disadvantage in attracting and retaining good staff. ⁴ In a report entitled 'Tomorrow's Workforce', published by the Hotel and Catering Training Company (HCTC), results of a survey showed that 'jobs in the industry are commonly rated by students as having lower status than jobs requiring similar skills and qualifications in other industries'. ⁵ The industry seems to be doing little to combat this perception. ⁶ The survey also showed that careers information available to students and young people making decisions about their future careers was inadequate and of poor quality.

3 *Implications explained*

5 *Comment – showing awareness of wider context*

6 *Link back to topic sentence and title, showing how main idea has developed*

5.6: What is a good conclusion? Activity

What are the reasons for staffing problems within the hotel and catering industry? Suggest ways these might be overcome.

1   The reader ends up with quite a good impression – better than the introduction promised. It looks as if this student did try to answer the question (*poor pay, unsocial hours*, etc.) at a basic level. The paragraph ends well: '*not necessarily be overcome but reduced*' (a 'Plus 1' comment; see Section 3.10). This goes right back to the title and redefines the writer's position in relation to it. However, the essay scores badly on the impression front: re-reading and editing would have sorted out the odd jump from the first sentence to the second, the spelling mistakes, and the crucial missing word.
Verdict: low average. Editing would have made a difference.

2 What's this? This is an arbitrary ending, not a conclusion. This essay ends mid-flow, deep into the discussion of a study being copied word for word (*our, us*) from some unreferenced source. The spelling mistakes which escaped the spellcheck (*intern* for *in turn*, *moral* for *morale*), and breathless, unpunctuated style reinforce the impression that the writer is not thinking – rather like the introduction. There is no evidence that this student has thought about the question or tried to answer it: an all-I-know-about answer.
Verdict: grade? I'm afraid I'd be harsh.

3 This essay ends rather as it began – bubbling with ideas that haven't found their place (the discussion on finance should have stayed in the body) and ends up looking waffly. This is a pity because this student has got a structure, and does answer the question. The paragraph starts with *staffing problems* (topic sentence) and ends with how to *overcome* them (concluding sentence).
Verdict: a reasonable average – but be tighter on structure in the future. Another reader may not want to hunt for the structure!

4 This paragraph is too short to draw the ideas of an essay to a conclusion. Nevertheless, at least it is on the right subject (which the introduction wasn't), even if it doesn't exactly answer the question. If you add a topic sentence (linking back to the title) it would do the job adequately. It has a 'Plus 1' thought at the end: *'better service for the customers'*.
Verdict: low to average grade.

5 This conclusion, like the introduction, is spot on, from the topic sentence, which uses the words of the title and adds a Plus 1 thought: *'up to the industry to make itself . . .'*. With the phrase *a combination of approaches,* it makes reference to the body of the essay without repeating it and adds the critique *no quick answer*. It ends with a link back to the topic sentence *labour supply,* which in turn links to the topic sentence of the introduction and the title.
Verdict: a pleasure to read. Good grade.

6 What question is this student answering? Something along the lines of 'How would you rate the hotel and catering industry as a future employer?' This, of course, is not what was asked. This is disappointing, given the competent introduction. Make sure you start and end on the title. The lapse in grammar (*prospective* for *prospects*) compounds the poor impression.
Verdict: Hmm. On the basis of this conclusion alone, you've answered the wrong question. Fail.

Developing Writing-Writing Essays

6 Essays are not the only way . . .

6.1 Other forms of writing

Essays are not the only way . . . of showing your knowledge and demonstrating your understanding of your subject. As we have seen, the essay is a particular form of academic writing with its own conventions. In other writing tasks you will still draw on the skills you have developed to meet the key criteria of essay writing:

- **answer the question**
- **structure your answer.**

When you are asked to present work in a different form, you will almost certainly be given clear and helpful guidelines on how to do it, and how you will be assessed. Make sure you take these on board.

You need to be clear about

- who you will be addressing – your audience
- what you are aiming to achieve – your purpose
- what you want to say – your message.

All this makes it easier to tailor your writing to the context you have been given and to the people who will be on the other end of your presentation.

Some of these forms are outlined below.

Reflective diary

This record of your learning is a private document with a public purpose. Unless it really is 'for your eyes only', take comments to this effect with a pinch of salt; this writing is 'private' in style, since you are the prime reader or audience, but 'public' in that, where it is a course requirement, it will be assessed. That said, it can be a rewarding form of writing, where you are assessed on the process of learning.

Portfolio

This is slightly more formal in style, but again an individual record providing evidence of your progress and achievements within your field. You have a great deal of scope as to how you present this, but, since you are going to be assessed on it, make sure you act on the guidance you have been given. Ask to see an example of work from past students if you are unclear about the format.

The less guidance you have about structure and form, the more you need to supply your own. A simple blueprint for this is to place on record different stages of your learning cycle: how you

- planned the activity
- carried it out
- reviewed and reflected on the experience
- drew conclusions, and used feedback from whatever source, to guide your planning for next time. The diagram on p. 5 shows how this structure was useful in planning this guide.

300-word essay

In this very short piece of writing, you need to be spot on about your key points. This is your outline essay plan (see Chapter 3) without the opportunity to explain, develop or illustrate beyond the minimum necessary to make your argument clear. It is a useful discipline. Think very hard about your topic sentences and conclusion.

Article

What is your purpose?

To inform? Explain? Persuade? Entertain?

Who is your audience?

Subject specialists? The general public? Students? Special interest groups?

Once you have answered these questions, you will know how to write. You then need to check out the conventions of this style of writing. Look in the library for published examples of writing for the audience you are aiming at and model your work on the structure and style they use.

Poster

Your work can be assessed literally at a glance on these two key criteria:

- answer the question

- structure your answer.

This is a demanding form of presentation. Below are the criteria one department set for a poster assessment:

```
Your poster will be read from about two feet away. It must

1 catch the looker's interest and quickly convey the central
  message

2 provide key details, central pieces of evidence to illustrate
  the central message

3 contribute to the plenary session, by showing how your study
  fits in to the broader topic.
```

Book review

This may be of a course text, or a book of your choice. You need to think carefully about readership:

- Who is your *review* for? Other students? Tutors? Practitioners?

- Who is the *book* for? Students? Tutors? Practitioners? How appropriate it is to this audience – in content, appearance, language, organization?

- What is the purpose of the text? To inform (introductory/specialist)? Explain? Persuade? Entertain?

You need to be clear about your criteria before you start, in order to judge how successful the book is in achieving its own objectives. Then judge: support each point with illustration, and draw conclusions your reader will find helpful.

Creative writing

There are all sorts of ingenious ways of prompting a serious critical response to an event, a situation, or other people's writings. These may be designed as

- **written pieces:** summary, letter, pamphlet, narrative

- **texts for spoken delivery:** lecture, dialogue, presentation of case, formal speech . . .

And there are plenty of other formats. Again, start from the guidance you have been given and look for models before you start.

6.2 Writing with a purpose

With all writing, it pays to do some strategic thinking:

- **What** exactly do I have to produce?

- **Why** am I writing? What do I hope to achieve?

- **Who** is it for? What does my reader – hypothetical or real – want?

before you get on to questions of process,

- **How? When? Where?**

When the forms in which you are asked to write are unusual, you are more likely to focus on these questions, but it is equally helpful to start with these for the old favourite – the essay. This is a form of academic writing with its own conventions and shorthand:

Yes, you have got a structure, but does it help you to answer the question? The conclusion suggests not.

Once you are clear about what these conventions and criteria are, you can develop the skills to deliver them. I hope you find this guide useful along the way.

Good luck!